ISLAMIST FOREIGN FIGHTERS RETURNING HOME AND THE THREAT TO EUROPE

HEARING

BEFORE THE

SUBCOMMITTEE ON EUROPE, EURASIA, AND EMERGING THREATS

OF THE

COMMITTEE ON FOREIGN AFFAIRS
HOUSE OF REPRESENTATIVES

ONE HUNDRED THIRTEENTH CONGRESS

SECOND SESSION

SEPTEMBER 19, 2014

Serial No. 113–217

Printed for the use of the Committee on Foreign Affairs

Available via the World Wide Web: http://www.foreignaffairs.house.gov/ or http://www.gpo.gov/fdsys/

U.S. GOVERNMENT PRINTING OFFICE

89–816PDF   WASHINGTON : 2014

For sale by the Superintendent of Documents, U.S. Government Printing Office
Internet: bookstore.gpo.gov   Phone: toll free (866) 512–1800; DC area (202) 512–1800
Fax: (202) 512–2104   Mail: Stop IDCC, Washington, DC 20402–0001

CONTENTS

ISLAMIST FOREIGN FIGHTERS RETURNING HOME AND THE THREAT TO EUROPE

FRIDAY, SEPTEMBER 19, 2014

House of Representatives,
Subcommittee on Europe, Eurasia, and Emerging Threats,
Committee on Foreign Affairs,
Washington, DC.

The subcommittee met, pursuant to notice, at 9:24 a.m., in room 2172, Rayburn House Office Building, Hon. Dana Rohrabacher (chairman of the subcommittee) presiding.

Mr. ROHRBACHER. I call this hearing to order.

And this is the Subcommitteeq on Europe, Eurasia, and Emerging Threats. And today we will be discussing an emerging threat to Europe, which is an area that we are focused on, but it is also an emerging threat to the world.

And I am going to handle things a little differently for this hearing. I am going to permit my—or ask my ranking member if he would move forward with his opening statement first.

I will then have my opening statement as chairman of the subcommittee, and I will ask my colleagues if—to have short opening statements as well.

I yield, then, to Mr. Keating.

Mr. KEATING. Thank you, Mr. Chairman, for holding this important and timely hearing.

I would like to also thank our esteemed witnesses, including Ms. Farah Pandith. And I am pleased that you are able to join us. Ms. Pandith's uncle, Dr. Ashraf, and I have a long history in Massachusetts, and I am so happy to see his legacy live on through his niece, who is testifying before us today.

Today's hearing is particularly relevant, given the geographic proximity of Europe to the conflict zone. Social networking, the internet, the propaganda have become the premier recruitment tools for terrorist gangs expanding their reach far into Europe and to the United States. These tools are cheap and effective. Even for the group like ISIL, who seems to have plentiful resources, they are being used. For this reason, I think that the nexus of our counterterrorism strategy should focus on various facets of their recruitment and communication strategy. This has been the root of the problem for decades and this is what we must attack.

Of course, we will need the cooperation of our transatlantic and regional partners to do this effectively. The National Counterterrorism Center estimates that as of this month, as many as 12,000 individuals have traveled to Syria since 2011 in order to support the armed militants there. This figure includes well over 1,000 European citizens and more than 100 Americans. The other estimates, particularly from our allies overseas, expect these numbers to be even higher.

Europe can serve as a barometer for what may come in the United States, and for this reason, we must continue to work closely with our European partners and find ways to facilitate better information-sharing and communication. The FBI and other intelligence agencies are already working with domestic and international partners to track foreign fighters traveling through the Mideast.

As such, interagency cooperation and information-sharing will undoubtedly be put to a test as agencies seek to coordinate and respond to this threat, particularly across international boundaries. For this reason, I for one will continue to be a strong advocate for incorporating local law enforcement into this framework and utilizing their force multiplier effect.

Yet as I mentioned earlier, there is a larger piece of the puzzle, and that is with the mindset and recruitment of these militants who come to their Western nations to join brutal gangs that go on to rape, kill and divide thousands, if not millions, comes into bear.

As a transatlantic community, we can only fight the lure of terrorism by determining its causes and devising appropriate countermeasures. In particular, I feel the messages being promoted, the heritage and the varied cultural history of the Middle East and North Africa will be important to helping young people to find their true identities instead of listening to backwards propaganda seeking to destroy that history.

Further, although controversial, I think it is important to reassess our partners in this fight. Are all the countries that have been affected and impacted by foreign fighter and this phenomenon doing what they can do to stem recruitment and financing? Are they protecting those in their own population and region from being coerced and harmed from these activities? A true partner in countering radicalism would not only do what they could do to curtail such activities from taking place abroad, but would have zero tolerance for extremism to go unchecked at home as well.

These are important questions to weigh when evaluating the capabilities of our international partners, who in most cases are more prone to attacks by radical groups than we are. Yet radicalization is occurring across the world in rural and urban settings, wealthy and poor communities, and among all education levels.

In the long-run, we must ensure that courses of action we pursue are not only targeting terrorist groups, but the polarizing policies that often lead to this kind of societal division.

Further, this composition now must include both genders, for it is not only men who take up arms, but women who play an integral role in the stabilization and organization of society within ISIL and as well as other extremist groups. Muslim women are growing up in increasingly conservative, closed environments, and this will have an effect on future generations.

The subject of today's hearing is of utmost concern to our own national security, and I look forward to hearing each of our witnesses' perspectives on this timely issue.

And with that, I thank the chairman and yield back.

Mr. ROHRBACHER. Well, thanks very much. And this morning's hear is on the merging threat of Islamist foreign fighters going to Syria and Iraq and the specific threat that they pose when they seek to return to Europe, and how does that impact us in the United States as well.

In 2011, the Syrian people rose up in revolt against their government. Over 3 years later, Syria has been torn apart by ethnic and sectarian strife. It is in ab open civil war. Radical Islamic terrorist groups, including al-Qaeda, have taken full advantage of this chaos. Possibly as many as 15,000 foreign fighters have entered Syria from around, well, perhaps 80 different countries to take up arms in this fight.

It appears that several thousand of those fighters came from Europe and hold passports from European countries. Many of these Islamists have joined ISIL, a heinous, brutal anti-Western terrorist organization that has grown to contest vast territory in both Syria and Iraq.

In ISIL, we face a terrorist group which controls land and has proven its abilities on the battlefield. It is also one of the richest terrorist groups in the world. They profit from criminal activity, extortion, black market oil sales, and of course the easy capture, or you might say gift, of vast amounts of American military equipment that we had generously provided Iraq. This is a mega-million-dollar operation on their part.

It is a nightmare to think about the kind of attacks ISIL could pull off, given their financial resources, their geographic safe havens and their access to so many recruits with Western passports.

The filmed beheading of James Foley and Steven Sotloff and David Haines tells us all that we need to know, that is all we need to know about the intentions of this terrorist organization. The terrorist holding the knife, and let us remember, the terrorist holding the knife in the beheading videos spoke with a British accent. That indicates the magnitude of the security challenge that we face.

We have already begun to see the threat of terrorism emanating from Syria. This week, a Yemen-born naturalized American citizen was indicted for attempting to provide support to ISIL in New York state. Dozens of people have also been arrested just this week in Australia and in the Balkans in connection to plots to aid ISIL and conduct terrorist attacks in the West.

And the words ''terrorist attacks in the West'' perhaps is a little too soft. Maybe we should understand what a terrorist attack in the West means are the bodies, the brutal tearing apart of the bodies of women and children, civilians, people who just want to live their lives. And this group of other human beings, for whatever reason they have, will at random murder our fellow citizens and people who live in Western countries. Perhaps, as we will hear from our witnesses, I would like to hear about their—what motive we are talking about here perhaps to terrorize Western civilization out of a huge section of the globe.

In May, a Muslim terrorist who held French citizenship and who had traveled to Syria, shot and killed four people in a Jewish museum in Brussels. Those victims, they were honest, ordinary people, could be related to any of us.

And during our discussions this morning, I hope to learn from the panelists about why ISIL's bloody message of hate and violence attracts far too many of European Muslims; what are the viable options for European countries in this situation to prevent terrorists from returning home; what attracts them to it, and how can we prevent them from coming back to their home countries and conducting this type of murder, horrible murder upon innocent people in our societies; how can we better work with our European allies; and, let me add, how can we better work with the European allies and Russia to defend ourselves against this shared threat?

Finally, let me just note that I think we would do well to learn from Europe's immigration experience as we talk about reforming our own laws. This problem is not only counterterrorism, but it is a question of how different people can fit together in a free society.

We have a lot to cover, so with that, I turn to my—the ranking member has already been heard from. Other members perhaps have short opening statements, and I yield to Judge Poe.

Mr. POE. Thank you, Mr. Chairman.

ISIS, as you have said, is a threat that we need to understand has to be reckoned with. I fear the West, especially the United States, underestimates them. They have, unlike many of the terrorist groups, set up governance in northern Iraq and in Syria. They tax the people, they govern the community, they have oil, they have money, and they are determined fighters. And, as you said, they have a lot of American equipment already.

The United States for years has supplied equipment to the Iraqis and tried to train them. In the first encounter with ISIS in northern Iraq, they cut and ran. A lot of Americans believe they just threw down some small arms and some MRE's and some ammo and took off running. Not so. Here is an M1 tank that the Iraqi Government was given by the United States. Confronted with ISIS, they bailed, and now ISIS controls an M1 tank belonging to the American citizens.

Here is the parade that they celebrated after capturing several Humvees abandoned by the Iraqis that we subsidized. And at the bottom, what to me is the most alarming: These are four Humvees, American-made, given to the Iraqi troops to fight ISIS, and after they cut and ran, they were abandoned, and now this is an ISIS truck headed to Syria to fight in Syria. I think we underestimate who these people are.

Foreign fighters for ISIS are already coming back to Europe and launching attacks. Monday, Germany held its first trial of an alleged German-born Jihadist. In May 2014, a terrorist affiliated with ISIS killed three people at the Jewish museum in Brussels. British Prime Minister David Cameron said last week that there have already been at least six planned terrorist attacks in the EU countries from ISIS. And the threat won't stay in Europe, as the Australians have already found out this week. Because they come from visa-waiver countries, many of these individuals are able to travel to the U.S.

We have to work with European friends to identify and track foreign Jihadists fighting in Syria. We also must convince them that this is a group to be reckoned with. They are a threat to all civilized peoples. They cannot be allowed to return home to continue their Jihad.

I have introduced H.R. 5406, the Foreign Terrorist Organization Passport Revocation Act, exactly for this purpose. This bill calls for the State Department to revoke U.S. passports for individuals who are fighters for any foreign terrorist organization or helping to support an FTO in any way.

American citizens that fight for ISIS are traitors, they are Benedict Arnolds, and they are not welcome back in the U.S.

And with that, Mr. Chairman, I will yield back.

Mr. ROHRBACHER. Thank you very much.

Mr. Yoho.

Mr. YOHO. Thank you, Mr. Chairman.

Witnesses, I appreciate you being here. This is a very important topic.

In lieu of what is going on in our world today, as Mr. Keating spoke, radical terrorist groups are growing around the world. It would be wise and prudent for us to address this before it gets any worse. And we have heard reports, suspected reports in this country of already things happening. You have got to worry about—or think about the Boston Marathon bombing. Is this the beginning of a way that is going to happen here that is unacceptable?

In lieu of what is going on in the Middle East, we talk about ISIL coming over here, and they even said they were coming to America, we have to pay attention and not allow that to happen. And it is—as I think they have to be dealt with over in a foreign country, we need to do more here to secure our borders. And I would like to hear ideas from you on securing our borders; not just the southwest border, but all of our borders, in addition to the passports that—people that have Western passports that travel over there.

In fact, we introduced a bill this week, it is called the Terrorist Nationality Act, that it sounds like other members have done too, that will strip citizenship away from people that have known affiliation with foreign terrorist groups or have picked up arms against American citizens or American military.

So I look forward to hearing suggestions on what we can do to make our country safer.

And with that, I yield back. Thank you.

Mr. ROHRBACHER. Well, thank you all very much.

We have two great witnesses with us, and we plan to have a great discussion with you after your testimony.

First, Thomas Joscelyn, a senior fellow with the Foundation for Defense of Democracies, and senior editor, of course, of The Long War Journal, a publication which tracks counterterrorism issues. He is a widely respected expert on al-Qaeda and its related groups around the world. He writes and contributes often to The Weekly Standard and makes guest appearances on television and radio. He has appeared before other Foreign Affairs, House Foreign Affairs Committee hearings, and we are pleased to welcome him to this subcommittee.

Also we have with us Ms. Farah Pandith, is the Fisher Family fellow at the Kennedy School of Government at Harvard University. She was appointed in 2009 as the first ever Special Representative to the Muslim Communities by Secretary of State Clinton. She worked in that capacity to engage and communicate with Muslim communities around the world on behalf of the United States Government. For her achievement, she was awarded the Secretary's Distinguished Honor Award in 2013.

Prior to her appointment, she held senior positions in the U.S. Agency for International Development and the State Department's Bureau of European and Euro-Asian Affairs. She has also worked as the Director of Middle East Regional Initiatives for the National Security Council. She has earned a master's degree from Fletcher School of Law and Diplomacy at Tufts University.

And I appreciate the witnesses. And I guess first we will hear from—it is a toss-up here. How about—how about if we go with Ms. Farah Pandith.

STATEMENT OF MS. FARAH PANDITH, FISHER FAMILY FELLOW, BELFER CENTER, HARVARD KENNEDY SCHOOL OF GOVERNMENT (FORMER U.S. SPECIAL REPRESENTATIVE TO MUSLIM COMMUNITIES)

Ms. PANDITH. Good morning. And thank you to the house—that would help.

Good morning, and thank you to the House Foreign Affairs Committee for inviting me here today.

Mr. Chairman and members of the Subcommittee on Europe, Eurasia, and Emerging Threats, it is my honor and pleasure to be here today for this important and timely hearing.

My name is Farah Pandith. I am a senior fellow at the Kennedy School of Government at Harvard University. My opinions and my written and verbal testimony are my own.

I have come before you today to talk about the threat of foreign fighters returning to Europe and what the United States could and should be doing about it. As a political appointee in the George W. Bush and Obama administrations, I spent a decade working on the impact of extremist ideologies on Muslim millenials, especially in Europe. I saw firsthand the complex processes by which extremists prey on young Muslims, tear apart local communities, and threaten stability worldwide.

In January of this year, I left government with the intention of writing a book that would explain what I had seen and what we can do to win the ideological war against extremism. I firmly believe we can win.

I am a proud American, and I know firsthand of the many men and women who serve our Nation with passion, commitment and steadfast determination to keep us safe from harm. I have been honored to work with and for them.

I also know the respect our Presidents have for all faiths. Both administrations under which I have served have openly stated that the heinous acts of terrorists do not, by any means, represent the religion of Islam.

My interest and involvement in the issue of extremism isn't typical. Out of college, I served in the George H.W. Bush administration, but left to attend the Fletcher School of Law in Diplomacy. It was there in 1993 that I focused on national security and was awarded a grant to travel to Kashmir during a very delicate and unstable time. I conducted interviews with militants, and began to understand the power of ideologies and the impact they were having on an older culture, heritage and a way of life.

I stayed in Massachusetts after graduate school, but felt called to serve after the events of 9/11. Al-Qaeda was trying to define my country and my religion. I could not sit back and watch.

For more than a decade since, I have worked closely on the issue of extremist ideologies impacts on Muslims. During my tenure at the National Security Council, the Danish cartoon crisis broke out. And in 2006, we found ourselves unprepared for the reality that something that happened in Copenhagen could have an effect on a life in Kabul.

Then Assistant Secretary for European and Eurasian Affairs, Dan Fried, asked me to serve as his senior advisor, to focus solely on Muslims in Europe and to help recalibrate the way our Embassies engaged with Muslims. Our country had never had that position, and Ambassador Fried understood how vital it was that we reach out more boldly to Muslims in Europe, gain an understanding of their diversity of experiences, and analyze the impact on them of extremist narratives.

For 2 years I traveled across Europe and met with Muslim communities, getting to know what was happening within communities and between generations and ethnicities. To push back against extremist narratives, we seeded several path-breaking initiatives that directly addressed the idealogical threat posed by extremists. These initiatives identified credible Muslim voices within Muslim communities, and by partnering with and supporting them, helped them to wield greater influence among young Muslims susceptible to extremist messages. Several of these CVE initiatives, such as Sisters Against Violent Extremism, continue to operate today independent of the U.S. Government.

The most vital fact I gleaned from thousands of conversations I had across Europe was that Muslim youths were having an identity crisis and that they were searching for answers. Extremist narratives were filling the intellectual vacuum created by this crisis, and governments were ill-equipped to deal with it.

A similar dynamic continues to unfold before our eyes with ever-more violent and gruesome implications.

In order for ISIL or other extremist organizations to persuade someone to join its army, these groups must be able to appeal emotionally to a young person eager for meaning and a sense of belonging.

This morning I want to make five points related to foreign fighters, their threat to us, and what America could be doing to fight back.

First, both men and women are at risk today. Just yesterday we saw in a new report that an Austrian teenage girl, who joined ISIL, is now pregnant. The presence of female recruits represents a new and important change in the extremist landscape.

Second, policymakers should be concerned not just with individuals who leave their home countries to fight in the Middle East or elsewhere, but with the ideology that continues to spread among those left behind.

Third, European civilization does not construct national identities in a uniform way. As a result, we must be local and nuanced in our policy approaches.

Fourth, we can win the ideological war with extremism by investing significantly in soft power.

Fifth, free borders in Europe don't represent the whole story. Free ideas bounce around the world online, keeping the cycle of hatred turning, but free ideas could also potentially feed a more virtuous cycle of peace and respect for others. With coordinated and comprehensive attention, we can dramatically change the patterns of discourse within Muslim communities, with positive consequences for Europe, the United States, and our allies.

Extremist ideology is the greatest threat of our time. The generation at risk is massive, global, and digitally connected. It is time we address the ideological threat head on and stop the recruitment from happening. This is winnable if we behave smartly, proactively, and creatively.

Thank you again for the opportunity to speak with you.

Mr. ROHRBACHER. Well, thank you very much. That was very thoughtful testimony, and I am sure we will have some serious questions for you.

[The prepared statement of Ms. Pandith follows:]

Hearing on

Islamist Foreign Fighters Returning Home and the Threat to Europe

Testimony by Farah Pandith

Senior Fellow, Future of Diplomacy Project, Kennedy School of Government

Before The Subcommittee on Europe, Eurasia and Emerging Threats

Foreign Affairs Committee of the United States House of Representatives, US Congress

September 19, 2014

Mr. Chairman and distinguished members of the subcommittee:

Thank you for inviting me to share my perspective and experience. My name is Farah Pandith. As of February 2014 I have been at Harvard University's Kennedy School of Government. The opinions I am expressing in both my written and verbal testimony are my own.

Almost five years ago today, I was sworn in as the first-ever Special Representative to Muslim Communities at the US Department of State. I served in this role for five years and traveled to more than 80 countries, where I met with thousands of Muslims. I engaged with communities, heard stories, and developed a new perspective on what is happening globally to Muslim youth.

The first thing to understand is that Muslim youth are experiencing a profound identity crisis unlike any in modern Islamic history. Nearly every day since September 12, 2001, Muslim Millennials have seen the word "Islam" or "Muslim" appear on the front pages of papers on and offline. They have grown up scrutinized because of their religion—and much of this attention is not positive. As a result, they are asking questions like: What does it mean to be modern and Muslim? What is the difference between culture and religion? Who speaks for my generation? While members of earlier generations might have turned to close-knit families and communities for help answering such questions, Millennials are unfortunately tuning in to unsavory figures encountered on the Internet and in other venues. Extremists prey on young Muslims and offer ready-made answers designed specifically to appeal to this generation. They market their ideas with savvy and alarming expertise—from magazines to apps, YouTube sermons to Hip Hop.

That is by no means all that's going on. Muslim women are becoming far more conservative across the planet, rejecting established, local traditions of dress and society. They are "veiling" when their mothers and grandmothers did not. They are listening to radical sermons on satellite TV beamed from Pakistan and Saudi Arabia. They are downloading music, poetry, and blogs that celebrate isolation and hatred of the "other." They are keeping their children away from people not "like them." And most recently, they are joining the armies of Al-Qaeda (AQ) and the Islamic State of Iraq and the Levant (ISIL). Because a mother is a child's first teacher, and because Muslim women are now showing a desire to be in the fight, young women are in a position to make or break their succeeding generation.

This summer, with its gruesome images of beheadings and other atrocities, has represented another turning point for our nation and other countries around the world. For the first time since 9/11, we are re-awakening emphatically to the growing threat posed by extremists. At the moment, we are rightfully concerned about the potential of radicalized youth returning from battlefields to conduct terrorist actions. But in addition to the short-term impacts on public safety, we should be concerned about the long-term ability of battle-hardened extremists to build new terrorist networks at home and extend existing ones by preying on youth. There is a critical ideological battle to be waged here. Extremists remain radicalized once they return. They are technologically savvy and understand how to use emotions to attract recruits. They also might command heightened and growing legitimacy in Muslim communities. Hard power responses such as retrieving passports are a start, but we need to do much more to prevent recruitment of new terrorists.

It's simple: If we clamp down on recruitment, then before too long, ISIL and others will not have armies. The radicalization of an individual is a gradual process: Why haven't we done more to intercede proactively during the initial stages of ideological persuasion? Why are we only interceding much later by attempting to stop extremists as they seek to cross national borders? Recruitment is a relatively new phenomenon, but we certainly possess enough information thirteen years after 9/11 to address the issue and scale up counter-measures at the local level, both in our country and around the world. We must decide if our goal is merely to stop an immediate threat, or to stop recruitment from happening in the first place.

The US government has struggled since 9/11 to wage a "war of ideas." This is understandable, since such a war throws us headlong into fundamental theological and social debates that we are not equipped to fight. The good news is that we *can* win a war of ideas with extremists. To do so, however, we must invest boldly and massively scale up its use of soft power. During the two years that I served as Senior Advisor in the EUR Bureau, we seeded many soft power initiatives and networks, demonstrating a proof of concept. Initiatives like Sisters Against Violent Extremism (SAVE) were designed in the image of Mothers Against Drunk Driving to be grassroots, local, and responsive. Recognizing that European Muslim youth were in need of positive role models, we created the first pan-European professional network that activated a new narrative and inspired others.

By partnering with individuals and community groups across Europe, we managed to lift up voices of Muslims who had influence within local neighborhoods and communities, establishing the basis for an empowering a grassroots *countermovement* in opposition of extremist manifestations. We joined former extremists, victims of terrorism, entrepreneurs, and women into layered networks dedicated to combatting the allure of the extremist narrative and ideology. This is the kind of work that we must now dramatically "scale up" if we are to prevail.

We can't create an ideological countermovement on the backs of a few isolated government-funded programs. It requires much broader commitment and focus starting now. Principles for future action should include:

- Investing significantly in soft power the way we did during the Cold War. We must give soft power as much credibility as we do hard power.

- Creating a comprehensive, coordinated strategy that does not skirt the ideological threat and that mobilizes all levers of power available to us (again, as we did during the Cold War). Such a strategy should incorporate lessons we've learned from the ground up, and it should invest in local answers.

- Adopting helpful and appropriate goals. The point here is not to win a popularity contest—to "win hearts and minds." Rather, it's to get voices online and offline to push back against what the extremists are selling. It's to flood the marketplace of ideas with online and offline counter-narratives articulated by Muslims themselves. Rather than simply disseminating our message ourselves, we need to act as convener, facilitator, and intellectual partner to Muslim youth, bringing together their great ideas and seeding them. This approach will hold far more credibility in Muslim communities.

- Publicly condemning countries like Saudi Arabia, Qatar, and others that are giving life to an eco system that ignites extremist ideology—through textbooks, radical preachers, and mosques that promote hate and reject the diversity of Muslims around the world (not to speak of other faiths).

- Emphasizing proactive attacks on extremist recruiting, not reactive and exponentially costlier "hard power" interventions once military threats have already materialized. Remember, without recruits, there are no troops.

- Ramping up initiatives and knowledge about the radicalization of women, and developing new approaches to mobilize them *against* radicalism.

- Creating awareness campaigns about radicalization the way we do for diseases like AIDS or breast cancer.

- Normalizing the conversation about extremism so that more private-sector money flows into soft power initiatives. Government can do this by sharing information about what we are seeing and convening helpful players outside of government.

- Anticipating extremist ideological attacks, and keeping an arsenal of strong counter-actions at the ready. In this field, there are few real surprises. With imagination we can predict the kind of tools extremists will use against us. We ought to be ready with swift responses, not wait days and weeks to react.

What I was asked to do at State during the Bush Administration was unique. At the time, forward-thinking policy-makers understood that America had to be proactive in engaging with Muslim communities in Europe. You might remember the intense days after the Danish Cartoon Crisis when everyone—our nation, as well as our European allies—was caught off-guard by the realization that something happening in Copenhagen could affect lives in Kabul. Sadly, these many years later, we have seen this phenomenon play out all too often. A false rumor, a video, a preacher threatening to burn the Quran can all unleash unrest as well as violence in faraway places such as Australia, Brazil, Zanzibar. We must accept that extremism *is* a global threat—that something happening in Copenhagen does have an effect on a life in Kabul.

The strategy of the extremists is evilly smart. By that I mean they are doing everything from all angles to re-make the world according to their apocalyptic vision. We understand this, but we are not doing enough to connect the dots and neutralize all their methods. Let me give just one example of how we might disempower extremists. In addition to the principles above, and as part of a larger strategy to counteract extremists intellectually, we should also take urgent steps to protect sacred and historical sites. ISIL and its ideological allies are not simply attempting to alter the political landscape and erase national borders; they are attempting to destroy entire peoples, histories, and cultures that threaten their worldview. They are getting rid of evidence that diversity exists, and with nothing to prove otherwise, generations going forward will only have *their* narrative.

As you are aware, extremists have been exiling and slaughtering ancient Christian communities in eastern Syria and northern Iraq; Shia, Kurdish, Sufis, and other minority families and towns; and Sunnis willing to oppose their nightmarish rule. The language of Jesus—Aramaic—is under direct and imminent threat as communities in Syria and Iraq who still speak its dialects are being killed or dispersed. And this problem is not isolated to Iraq or Syria; it's part of a greater tragedy unfolding from Central and South Asia to West Africa.

ISIL is hardly the first to use cultural destruction to demoralize their enemies, finalize their victories, and reshape history. The glorious cartouches on the walls in the Valley of the Kings in Egypt show scratched-out dynastic rulers whose names were replaced by those of new Pharaohs. Invading Mongols destroyed libraries and infrastructure across the Middle East, including the great libraries of Baghdad in 1258. The Nazis burned books and great works of art. Yet with the rise of extremism, cultural destruction appears to have found new importance as a tactic. In 2001, the world watched as the Taliban destroyed The Great Buddhas and hundreds of shrines in Bamiyan Province in Afghanistan. In 2006, in Iraq's destruction of the Shia mosque in Samarra, AQ helped spark sectarian fighting and destruction in Iraq. Sufi graves and shrines have been destroyed from Tunisia and Libya to the Balkans and Bahrain. The Pakistan Taliban has attacked Ahmadi minorities and their mosques. In 2013, hard-line Islamists in Mali destroyed numerous mausoleums and burned ancient Islamic manuscripts in the fabled libraries of Timbuktu. Radical Salafis in Egypt have even suggested destroying the Sphinx and the Pyramids because they are "un-Islamic."

As part of the ideological battle underway, allied extremists are trying to reshape the very identity of people based on a distorted view of Islam. The United States and its partners need to act to save persecuted minorities, sacred sites and priceless historical artifacts. Preservation of history *materially contradicts the extremist narrative* and testifies to our own record of tolerance and inclusiveness. In the course of protecting sacred and historical sites, we also are able to protect the peoples and heritage attached to such sites. Finally, amid sectarian tension, protection of sites helps avoid flashpoints of confessional conflict and could create opportunities for cooperation and goodwill.

We are fortunate to posses a set of actors and networks already committed to and working on the preservation of peoples, texts, and culture, including leading archaeologists, anthropologists, universities, heritage trusts, museums and libraries, and even activist celebrities. We could make great headway by mobilizing these assets in innovative ways. For instance,

- Our government could fund the Smithsonian and leading museums to preserve ancient texts and assist libraries and networks of collectors to move precious texts at risk.

- Western churches and congregations could adopt sister parishes or communities under assault in the Middle East, providing funding for refugees and protection of ancient churches and monasteries. Social media could be used to raise awareness and funding in real time.

- We could launch real-time mapping and monitoring of at-risk sites, much as George Clooney's Satellite Sentinel project and the Google Earth/Holocaust Museum website focused on the Sudan are already doing.

- The UN could consider positioning peace-keeping forces to protect villages and sites where feasible. Such forces capably defend diplomatic posts, personnel, and oil installations in conflict zones. Forces already invested in counter-terrorism—like the French in North Africa or the Kurds in northern Iraq—could take the lead in the defense management of such sites.

Countering extremist attempts to re-write history is just one of the many things we must do comprehensively across all channels in order to destroy their ability to recruit young Muslims. Extremism poses an obvious terrorist threat, but as I've argued, the way to engage this threat most effectively over the long-term is by emphasizing *ideological* means as a complement to hard power. We *can* beat extremists at their own game. We can end their exploitation of the Muslim identity crisis and beat back groups like Al Qaeda and ISIL at their source. Doing so won't cost a fraction of traditional hard power solutions, but it will require that we take a more entrepreneurial and innovative approach to policymaking. We must stop playing catch-up and get ahead of trends. We must connect the dots and not look at specific conflicts or extremist groups as if they are "one-offs." As a nation, we move swiftly, like nimbler start-ups. We defeated communist ideology during the Cold War by mustering creativity and full-on dedication. We can and must do this again.

One thing is certain: If we do not engage in the war of ideas for a generation, America, Europe, the world will continue to face extremist threats that will morph in shape and scope and grow ever more organized and dangerous. The time to act is now. So what are we waiting for?

#######

N.B. I am also submitting "Foreign Fighters; The Challenge of Counter-Narratives" by Rachel Briggs and Ross Frenett of the Institute for Strategic Dialogue in London, UK.

Mr. ROHRBACHER. And now to our next witness, and senior fellow with the Foundation for Defense of Democracies. You may proceed, Dr.—or Mr. Thompson.

Mr. JOSCELYN. Thank you, Congressman.

Mr. ROHRBACHER. Dr., but it is Mr.

Mr. JOSCELYN. No. It is Mr. all the way.

Mr. ROHRBACHER. Okay. Mr. Joscelyn.

STATEMENT OF MR. THOMAS JOSCELYN, SENIOR FELLOW, FOUNDATION FOR DEFENSE OF DEMOCRACIES

Mr. JOSCELYN. Well, thank you for having me here today to talk about this issue.

We have been tracking the issue of foreign fighters going to Syria at The Long War Journal for a while now, a few years going back to really late 2011, early 2012. And it is really stunning to me that today we have more foreign fighters in Syria than were in Afghanistan during the height of the Jihad against the Soviets. That is really an incredible metric if you think about it. And this creates all sorts of security challenges, of course.

I have a little bit of a nuanced view of this. We are right to be concerned about the threat the foreign fighters pose to the West and the possibility of using terrorist attacks. Most of them, however, will not come back our way. Most of them are going to remain invested in the fight in Iraq and Syria. Most of—some of them will even become disillusioned. And for those—some that become disillusioned, they can become partners for us in sort of counter-messaging to basically dispel the mythology that sort of the Jihad in Syria is some grandiose sort of quest, that they can actually become sort of our messengers in Europe and the West to tell people that going off to fight in Syria is not as great as the recruiters make it to sound out to be.

However, I want to say this. As the number of foreign fighters increases, there are two main problems: One, you can have sort of these acts of violence like the shooting at the museum in Brussels that you mentioned, Congressman, where we don't know if he was under direction of any senior terrorists or not, but it is still a serious threat that you can have somebody who is really known as a psychopath can basically go back to Europe.

And to your point, Congressman Yoho, about identifying these individuals who are traveling around, he traveled all throughout Europe through multiple Nations before that attack, and he had been identified by French intelligence in 2013 as a risk, and was still able to move around quite freely up until that day of terror. So we have that sort of threat.

The second level full threat is a more nuanced one that I think we really have to think about, which is if you think back to pre-9/11 Afghanistan, between 10 and 20,000 recruits went through al Qaeda's training camps in Afghanistan. What al-Qaeda was doing was they were trying to identify sort of the most talented and most dedicated recruits to re-purpose for attacks in the West, and that is what ultimately gave us, for example, the Hamburg cell that traveled from Germany to Afghanistan. These are individuals who are identified as being totally committed, skilled and somebody they could train up to basically fly planes into buildings.

What is interesting about that is those recruits who traveled to Afghanistan were originally wanted to actually go wage Jihad in Chechnya against the Russian Government. They weren't actually recruited originally to go fly planes into buildings in the U.S. This is how a Jihad in Afghanistan or elsewhere could be re-purposed very quickly and come back at us.

And so as the talent level of foreign fighters increases, what happens is that the skilled professional terrorists, the guys who I am really worried about, are basically sifting through the pile to figure out who is really the best recruits for them to use in operations against us.

U.S. officials say that the Islamic State doesn't pose an imminent threat to the U.S. homeland in terms of catastrophic attacks. The consensus seems to be that they don't—are not able to plan catastrophic terrorist attacks in the West at the moment. I would pause on that. History tells us that these threats evolve very, very quickly. Al-Qaeda in the Iranian peninsula went from a regional national insurgency to a direct threat against the U.S. homeland within a matter of basically 9 months, 9, 10 months, something along those lines.

There is a lot we don't know. We didn't know that Khalid Sheikh Mohammed, the mastermind of 9/11, was in fact an al-Qaeda operative until several months after 9/11. Okay?

So what worries me is what we don't about this group and its capabilities. We know the intent is there. And just because we don't think they have the ability to attack us in a catastrophic way right now in the West doesn't mean that they won't be able to in the near future.

But finally, I will say this: Everybody is rightfully concerned about ISIL, as we call it here right now, and the threat. It is sort of amazing to watch a rampage across two nation states. But, again, I have a slightly different view. I think the greater near term threat to us is actually—are actually the al-Qaeda operatives in Syria right now, who U.S. intelligence officials, European intelligence officials are very worried about planning catastrophic attacks against us.

These are guys who are embedded within Jabhat al-Nusra, which is an initial branch of al-Qaeda, and is actually a rival of ISIL inside Syria today. This is how complicated this is. The threat streams are coming from multiple directions. It is not just ISIL.

Within Jabhat al-Nusra, you have skilled operatives who are dispatched by Ayman al-Zawahir, the head of al-Qaeda, to Syria. And what they are doing is very carefully sorting through the pile of European and Western recruits to figure out who they can use, like the Hamburg cell for 9/11, something along those lines. That is a bigger near term concern, I think, in terms of big sort of spectacular terrorist attacks.

A big problem there too is that Jabhat al-Nusra is deeply embedded within the Syrian insurgency against the Assad regime. They are very popular amongst other rebels. They are not—this is—I know—I realize that yesterday I think there was big vote, of course, on funding and training the rebels. I—my one caveat there is we have got to be worried about how these rebels interact with

Jabhat al-Nusra. They are not ISIL. Okay. They are opposed to ISIL, they are opposed to Assad, and yet they are al-Qaeda. Right?

So this is a very complicated game that we have to play here and be worried about, and I don't hear a lot of discussion about that. And I am worried about that. That doesn't mean I necessarily oppose what the administration wants to do; it is just my own sort of—you know, we have to be very careful about how we do it. And we can get into that a little bit more during questioning, maybe.

Finally, back to your point, Congressman Yoho, about these recruits traveling. There was a suicide bomber for Jabhat al-Nusra earlier this year, who blew himself up, an American, known as Abu Salha, and he actually—this is, again, one of those things that worries me. He managed to travel to and from his home in Florida from the Jihad in Syria as he was basically being indoctrinated and recruited to blow himself up in Syria.

Now, Jabhat al-Nusra decided not to try and use him in an attack against the West, but you can bet that they learned from how he got in and out of the country what they can try and—and try and use that information in the future. And that is really, I think, how we should be thinking about that.

Thank you.

Mr. ROHRBACHER. Well, thank both of you for providing us that testimony.

[The prepared statement of Mr. Joscelyn follows:]

Congressional Testimony

"Islamist Foreign Fighters Returning Home and the Threat to Europe"

Thomas Joscelyn
Senior Fellow, Foundation for Defense of Democracies
Senior Editor, The Long War Journal

Hearing before House Committee on Foreign Affairs Subcommittee on Europe, Eurasia, and Emerging Threats

Washington, DC
September 19, 2014

FOUNDATION FOR
DEFENSE OF DEMOCRACIES

1726 M Street NW • Suite 700 • Washington, DC 20036

Chairman Rohrabacher, Ranking Member Keating and members of the Committee, thank you for inviting me here today to discuss the threat posed by Islamist foreign fighters returning home to Europe. We have been asked to answer the question, "How are European countries addressing the threat, and how can the US assist in those efforts to thwart future terrorist attacks?" I offer my thoughts in more detail below.

But I begin by recalling the 9/11 Commission's warning with respect to failed states. "In the twentieth century," the Commission's final report reads, "strategists focused on the world's great industrial heartlands." In the twenty-first century, however, "the focus is in the opposite direction, toward remote regions and failing states." A few sentences later, the Commission continues:

> If, for example, Iraq becomes a failed state, it will go to the top of the list of places that are breeding grounds for attacks against Americans at home. Similarly, if we are paying insufficient attention to Afghanistan, the rule of the Taliban or warlords or narcotraffickers may reemerge and its countryside could once again offer refuge to al Qaeda, or its successor.[1]

Those words were written more than a decade ago. Unfortunately, they still ring true today, not just for the US, but also for Europe. Except, we no longer have to worry about just Iraq becoming a failed state. We now have to contend with a failed state in Syria as well. And Syria is not "remote." It is much easier for foreign fighters to travel to Syria today than it was for new jihadists to get to Afghanistan in the 1980s. This is one reason that there are likely more foreign fighters in Syria than there were in Afghanistan at the height of the jihad against the Soviets. Estimates vary, but the total number of foreign recruits in Syria easily tops 10,000. A CIA source recently told CNN "that more than 15,000 foreign fighters, including 2,000 Westerners, have gone to Syria." They "come from more than 80 countries."[2]

This, of course, is an unprecedented security challenge and one that counterterrorism and intelligence officials will be dealing with for some time to come. It requires exceptional international cooperation to track the threats to Europe and elsewhere emerging out of Iraq and Syria. My thoughts below are focused on what I consider to be some of the key aspects of dealing with this threat.

At the moment, most people are understandably focused on the Islamic State (often called the Islamic State of Iraq and the Levant, ISIL, or ISIS). There is certainly a strong possibility that some foreign fighters will return from fighting in the Islamic State's ranks to commit an act of terror at home, either on their own accord or under the direction of senior terrorists.

However, I also want to focus our attention today one of the other significant threat streams coming out of Syria. Al-Qaeda's official branch in the country, Jabhat al-Nusrah, has experienced al-Qaeda veterans in its ranks. I think they pose more of a near-term threat when it

---

[1] US National Commission on Terrorist Attacks upon the United States, "The 9/11 Commission Report: Final Report of the National Commission on Terrorist Attacks Upon the United States," July 22, 2004, page 367.
[2] Jomana Karadsheh, Jim Sciutto & Laura Smith-Spark, "How Foreign Fighters Are Swelling ISIS Ranks in Startling Numbers," *CNN*, September 14, 2014. (http://www.cnn.com/2014/09/12/world/meast/isis-numbers/)

comes to launching catastrophic attacks in the West than do their Islamic State counterparts. And even though al-Nusrah and the Islamic State have been at odds, we should not rule out the possibility that parts of each organization could come together against their common enemies in the West. Indeed, two of al-Qaeda's leading branches are currently encouraging the jihadists in Syria to broker a truce, such that they focus their efforts against the US and its allies.[3] There is also a large incentive for terrorists in both organizations to separately lash out at the West, portraying any such attacks as an act of retaliation for the American-led bombings.

In my opinion, the key issues that officials in Europe and the US will continue to address include the following:

- **Throughout much of the war in Syria, Turkey has had an open door policy for jihadist and non-jihadist fighters alike.[4]**

  Turkey is not only a crucial transit point for jihadists entering Syria, it is also a common facilitation point for those returning to their home countries. European and American officials must continue to explore ways to put pressure on Turkey to disrupt the flow of foreign fighters and also convince the government to share as much intelligence as possible. Counterterrorism officials are most interested in intelligence identifying the fighters, recruiters, travel facilitators, financiers, arms distributors, and others.

- **Turkey's policy of distinguishing between the Islamic State and other extremists, including Jabhat al-Nusrah, an official branch of al-Qaeda, has been a failure.**

  While Turkey has been willing to work against the Islamic State, it has been far more accommodating when it comes to al-Nusrah and other extremist organizations. There have been occasional reports that the Turkish government has moved against al-Nusrah or other jihadists affiliated with the group. But this is not a consistent policy. Recently, the former American ambassador to Ankara, Francis Riccardione, told reporters that Turkey has been working with al-Nusrah. "We ultimately had no choice but to agree to disagree," Riccardione said. "The Turks frankly worked with groups for a period, including al Nusra[h], who we finally designated as we're not willing to work with."[5] Turkey opposed the US government's decision to designate al-Nusrah as a terrorist organization in late 2012.[6] And *The Wall Street Journal*, citing "officials involved in the internal discussions" surrounding the designation, even reported that the move was intended "to send a message to Ankara about the need to

---

[3] Thomas Joscelyn, "Al Qaeda Branches Urge Jihadist Unity against US," *The Long War Journal*, September 16, 2014. (http://www.longwarjournal.org/archives/2014/09/al_qaeda_branches_ur.php)

[4] For a summary of reports on Turkey's role in facilitating the flow of jihadists into Syria, see: Jonathan Schanzer, "Terrorism Finance in Turkey: A Growing Concern," *Foundation for Defense of Democracies*, February 2014, pages 8-10.
(http://www.defenddemocracy.org/content/uploads/documents/Schanzer_Turkey_Final_Report_3_smaller.pdf)

[5] Richard Spencer & Raf Sanchez, "Turkish Government Co-operated with al-Qaeda in Syria, Says Former US Ambassador," *The Telegraph* (UK), September 12, 2014.
(http://www.telegraph.co.uk/news/worldnews/europe/turkey/11093478/Turkish-government-co-operated-with-al-Qaeda-in-Syria-says-former-US-ambassador.html)

[6] US Department of State, Press Statement, "Terrorist Designations of the al-Nusrah Front as an Alias for al-Qa'ida in Iraq," December 11, 2012. (http://www.state.gov/r/pa/prs/ps/2012/12/201759.htm)

more tightly control the arms flow."[7] Furthermore, the US Treasury Department has recognized Turkey as a key link between al-Qaeda's Iran-based network, Gulf donors, and operatives in Syria. In October 2012, Treasury reported that al-Qaeda's Iran-based network is "working to move fighters and money through Turkey to support al-Qa'ida-affiliated elements in Syria" and the head of that network at the time was also "leveraging his extensive network of Kuwaiti jihadist donors to send money to Syria via Turkey."[8]

Turkey, therefore, is a key chokepoint for disrupting al-Qaeda's international terrorist network, including any terrorist plots aimed at the West.

- **Inside Syria today, al-Qaeda operatives in Jabhat al-Nusrah are already attempting to identify new recruits capable of striking the West.**

    US officials have warned of these efforts. "In Syria, veteran al Qaeda fighters have traveled from Pakistan to take advantage of the permissive operating environment and access to foreign fighters," the director of the National Counterterrorism Center (NCTC), Matthew Olsen, said during a speech earlier this month. Olsen added, "They are focused on plotting against the West."[9] The *Associated Press* recently reported that a cell of al-Qaeda operatives known as the "Khorasan group" has been sent to Syria "by Al Qaeda leader Ayman al Zawahiri to recruit Europeans and Americans whose passports allow them to board a US-bound airliner with less scrutiny from security officials."[10] Al-Qaeda operatives inside Syria are working with bomb makers from al-Qaeda in the Arabian Peninsula (AQAP), a branch of al-Qaeda that has proven to be particularly adept at placing explosives on board airliners. Al-Qaeda has English-speaking recruiters inside Syria who are capable of indoctrinating new recruits.[11] And some senior al-Qaeda operatives dispatched from Pakistan to Syria openly pine for attacks against the US homeland and American interests elsewhere on their widely-read Twitter accounts.[12]

    Thus, there is a clear and present danger that al-Qaeda will be able to successfully recruit new cells dedicated to attacking the West. Even if they assemble such cells, al-Qaeda will still have to get around the West's significant counterterrorism defenses. Still, the potential threat looms.

- **Most of the foreign fighters who travel from Europe to Syria will not become threats to**

---

[7] Adam Entous & Joe Parkinson. "Turkey's Spymaster Plots Own Course on Syria," *The Wall Street Journal*, October 10, 2013. (http://online.wsj.com/news/articles/SB10001424052702303643304579107373585228330)
[8] US Department of the Treasury, Press Release, "Treasury Further Exposes Iran-Based Al-Qa'ida Network," October 18, 2012. (http://www.treasury.gov/press-center/press-releases/Pages/tg1741.aspx)
[9] Matthew G. Olsen, "Remarks as Prepared," *The Brookings Institution*, September 3, 2014. (http://www.dni.gov/files/documents/2014-09-03%20Remarks%20for%20the%20Brookings%20Institution.pdf)
[10] Ken Dilanian & Eileen Sullivan. "Al Qaeda Group Could Be a Threat to US Aviation," *Associated Press*, September 14, 2014. (http://www.bostonglobe.com/news/world/2014/09/13/qaeda-cell-syria-could-pose-threat-aviation/GnqIdES9Ar4DZjTfbZvGXI/story.html)
[11] Thomas Joscelyn, "Al Qaeda Official in Syria Eas Extremist Preacher in Australia," *The Long War Journal*, March 21, 2014. (http://www.longwarjournal.org/archives/2014/03/former_islamic_preac.php)
[12] Thomas Joscelyn, "Treasury Designates 2 'Key' al Qaeda Financiers," *The Long War Journal*, August 22, 2014. (http://www.longwarjournal.org/archives/2014/08/treasury_designates_3.php)

their native or adopted home countries in the West. However, as the total number of foreign fighters increases, so does the probability that *some* of them will be repurposed for mass casualty attacks. Identifying the most "talented" and dedicated jihadist recruits should be a top priority.

Most of the foreign fighters who travel abroad will stay invested in the fight in Iraq and Syria. Others will become disillusioned and return home, realizing that the jihad is not as glamorous as it was made out to be. But as the number of foreign fighters increases, so does the talent pool available to professional terrorists interested in planning devastating terrorist attacks in the West.

Consider pre-9/11 Afghanistan. The overwhelming majority of al-Qaeda's recruits did not travel to Afghanistan to learn how to attack inside Europe or the US. Most of them fought inside Afghanistan, or were trained to fight in insurgencies elsewhere around the world. The 9/11 Commission found that between 10,000 and 20,000 recruits were trained in al-Qaeda-sponsored training camps between 1996 and September 11, 2001. [13] Only "a small percentage" of those recruits "went on to receive advanced terrorist training."[14] Of course, that "small percentage" of new jihadists included the suicide hijack pilots responsible for the 9/11 attacks. Al-Qaeda's leaders recognized that, among all their recruits, the terrorists in the Hamburg cell possessed the right combination of aptitude, Westernized habits, and travel documents to carry out a 9/11-style attack.

Disillusioned foreign fighters can be a good source of intelligence concerning which jihadists are the most capable and committed. European officials likely use something akin to an informant network within the jihadists' ranks already. Such efforts help determine, albeit imperfectly, the difference between jihadi tourists and the true believers. American and European officials must share any such intelligence.

Past experience has shown that jihadists recruited in Europe can be used in attacks on the US, and American jihadists can be used in plots against European countries. A noteworthy example of the latter is the story of David Headley's career. Headley, an American, performed surveillance for the 2008 Mumbai attacks. Al-Qaeda also considered using him in a plot against the Danish newspaper that published controversial cartoons of the Prophet Mohammed.

- **The Islamic State may or may not currently have the operational capability to launch mass casualty attacks in the West. But counterterrorism officials should constantly reassess their assumptions regarding the organization's reach.**

Counterterrorism officials say they have no intelligence indicating that the Islamic State is currently planning attacks inside the US. Indeed, the group *may* not currently have the capability to carry out a large-scale attack in the West. However, the past offers us some reasons for concern.

---

[13] The 9/11 Commission Report, page 67.

[14] US National Commission on Terrorist Attacks upon the United States, "Overview of the Enemy," Staff Statement No. 15, page 10. (http://www.9-11commission.gov/staff_statements/staff_statement_15.pdf)

We've learned that jihadist groups can quickly evolve from a national or regional insurgency into a threat against the US homeland. Al-Qaeda in the Arabian Peninsula (AQAP) was re-established in early 2009. On Christmas Day that year, a would-be suicide bomber nearly destroyed a Detroit-bound plane. Prior to that attack, AQAP wasn't considered a threat to the US homeland, as counterterrorism officials believed the group only posed a threat to US interests inside Yemen.[15] The same can be said for the Pakistani Taliban, which trained a man to plant a car bomb in the middle of Times Square. Both attempts luckily failed.

While not all jihadist organizations will target the US, some of them will. And they can quickly become a direct threat to the US homeland. We should keep in mind that the presence of highly-skilled bomb makers within AQAP was not known until after their bombs were deployed. It also wasn't known that Khalid Sheikh Mohammed, the architect of 9/11, was an al-Qaeda operative until several months after his minions carried out their deeds in New York, Washington, and Pennsylvania.

None of this is to suggest that we know the Islamic State is capable 9/11-style attacks today. The group is embroiled in a multi-sided fight in both Iraq and Syria, and this uses up much of its resources. But the lessons of the past are clear: The threat posed by the Islamic State can evolve quickly, and there is likely much we currently do not know. As NCTC director Matthew Olsen recent remarked, while counterterrorism officials have "no credible information that [the Islamic State] is planning to attack the" US, the group "has the potential to use its safe haven to plan and coordinate attacks in Europe and the US."[16]

- **The Islamic State's leaders have directly threatened the US, and we should take their threats seriously, even if we are not sure about their capabilities.**

In his very first recorded speech, Abu Bakr al-Baghdadi, the head of the Islamic State, threatened the US. Addressing American officials directly in an audio recording released on July 21, 2012, Baghdadi said: "As for your security, your citizens cannot travel to any country without being afraid. The mujahideen have launched after your armies, and have swore to make you taste something harder than what Usama had made you taste. You will see them in your home, Allah permitting. Our war with you has only begun, so wait."[17] In January of this year, Baghdadi promised the US that it would soon be in a "direct confrontation." Baghdadi again addressed America directly, saying, "So as to let you know, you the protector of the cross, that the war of agency will not enrich you in Syria as it did not enrich you in Iraq, and very soon you will be in the direct confrontation - you will be forced to do so, Allah permitting. The sons of the Islam have settled their selves for this day."[18]

---

[15] Thomas Joscelyn, "The System Failed," *The Weekly Standard*, May 19, 2010. (http://www.weeklystandard.com/blogs/system-failed)

[16] Matthew G. Olsen, "Remarks as Prepared," *The Brookings Institution*, September 3, 2014. (http://www.dni.gov/files/documents/2014-09-03%20Remarks%20for%20the%20Brookings%20Institution.pdf)

[17] "ISI Leader Champions Mission, Calls for Support in First Audio Speech," *SITE Intelligence Group*, July 21, 2012.

[18] "ISIL Leader Addresses Factional Conflict in Syria, Challenges U.S.," *SITE Intelligence Group*, January 19, 2014.

The beheadings of two American reporters and one British citizen in recent weeks have highlighted just how aggressively anti-Western the Islamic State is. In each of the three gruesome videos, the Islamic State's executioner makes it clear that group is opposed to the US-led bombing campaign. The Islamic State almost certainly had the desire to strike in US and Europe even prior to the bombings, but with the West becoming involved in the fight, the group may now make attacks abroad more of a priority.

- **There are clear warning signs that the Islamic State and its sympathizers already threaten Europe. The Islamic State has a worldwide network of supporters, with known operatives throughout Europe.**

The jihadist thought to be responsible for the May 24, 2014 shooting at the Jewish Museum of Belgium spent months in Syria.[19] Four people were killed in his attack. One of the hostages held by the Islamic State has identified Mehdi Nemmouche, the alleged shooter, as being responsible for torturing the group's prisoners in Syria.[20] Even if the Islamic State's leadership did not order Nemmouche to carry out an attack at the Jewish Museum, or on any other target, the shooting demonstrates the ability of a known jihadist to carry out a small-scale assault after returning from Syria. French counterterrorism officials had already deemed Nemmouche to be a risk, reportedly placing him under surveillance after he returned from Syria in 2013.[21] This should be considered a disturbing precedent, as Nemmouche was not an unknown at the time of his attack.

My colleague at *The Long War Journal*, Lisa Lundquist, has provided an excellent overview of the efforts made by counterterrorism officials in Europe and elsewhere to track and disrupt the Islamic State's international network.[22] The Islamic State currently has the capacity to carry out smaller-scale attacks in Europe, if its operatives can evade counterterrorism defenses.

- **The Islamic State's predecessor organizations first posed a threat to Europe more than a decade ago. While the organization has evolved significantly since then, current counterterrorism efforts should be seen as a continuation of the past, recognizing that some of the same recruiting and facilitation networks have likely been involved the whole time.**

Even before the Iraq War began in March 2003, the CIA was hunting suspected terrorists in Europe who were tied to al-Qaeda's operations in northern Iraq. The suspected terrorists worked in conjunction with Abu Musab al-Zarqawi, the founder of al-Qaeda in Iraq, which eventually evolved into the Islamic State. Former CIA director George Tenet writes in his

---

[19] Anne Penketh, "French Suspect in Brussels Jewish Museum Attack Spent Year in Syria," *The Guardian* (U.K.), June 1, 2014. (http://www.theguardian.com/world/2014/jun/01/french-suspect-brussels-jewish-museum-attack-syria)
[20] Kevin Rawlinson, "Jewish Museum Shooting Suspect 'Is Islamic State Torturer'," *The Guardian* (U.K.), September 6, 2014. (http://www.theguardian.com/world/2014/sep/06/jewish-museum-shooting-suspect-islamic-state-torturer-brussels-syria)
[21] Anne Penketh, "Brussels Jewish Museum Shooting: Suspect with Islamist Links Arrested," *The Guardian* (U.K.), June 1, 2014. (http://www.theguardian.com/world/2014/jun/01/suspect-arrest-brussels-jewish-museum-shooting)
[22] Lisa Lundquist, "The Islamic State's Global Reach," *The Long War Journal's Threat Matrix*, September 5, 2014. (http://www.longwarjournal.org/threat-matrix/archives/2014/09/the_islamic_state_and_the_sham.php)

autobiography that US officials' "efforts to track activities emanating from Kurmal [in northern Iraq] resulted in the arrest of nearly one hundred Zarqawi operatives in Western Europe planning to use poisons in operations."[23] Tenet notes that in the summer of 2000 al-Qaeda worked with Kurdish Islamists, including Ansar al-Islam, "to create a safe haven for al-Qaeda in an area of northeastern Iraq not under Iraqi government control, in the event Afghanistan was lost as a sanctuary."[24] The area became a "hub for al Qaeda operations" and "up to two hundred al Qaeda fighters began to relocate there in camps after the Afghan campaign began in the fall of 2001."[25] Tenet also writes that two longtime subordinates to Ayman al-Zawahiri, Thirwat Shihata and Yussef Dardiri, were among the "dozen al Qaeda-affiliated extremists" who "converged on Baghdad, with apparently no harassment on the part of the Iraqi government" in 2002.[26] The CIA had "[c]redible information" that Shihata "was willing to strike US, Israeli, and Egyptian targets sometime in the future."[27] Dardiri, also known as Abu Ayyub al-Masri, went on to become one of the first leaders of the Islamic State of Iraq, which became the current Islamic State. Dardiri was killed in April 2010. Shihata was arrested in Egypt earlier this year.

The threats continued in the years that followed. The Department of Homeland of Security announced in 2004 that al-Qaeda in Iraq (AQI) was ordered by Osama bin Laden to assemble a cell capable of attacking the US. In 2007, failed attacks in London and Glasgow were tied back to AQI.

In sum, while for many the threat posed by the Islamic State appears to be a new phenomenon, it is actually the continuation of a story that dates back to late 2001.

---

[23] George Tenet, *At the Center of the Storm: My Years at the CIA*, (New York: HarperCollins Publishers, 2007), page 351.
[24] Tenet, page 350.
[25] *Ibid.*
[26] Tenet, page 351.
[27] *Ibid.*

Mr. ROHRBACHER. Again, I will yield to my ranking member, and I will just top things off after we give Congressman Yoho a chance to ask some questions as well.

Mr. KEATING. Thank you, Mr. Chairman.

Thank you both for your testimony. I think we are seeing in a continuum, from the inception of ideology to how they are practically carrying many of these things out. That was very clear in both of your testimonies, and I appreciate that.

I want to focus in for a moment on a shared commitment I have with the administration to strengthen women's rights globally and to empower women and their families in transitional societies, such as Iraq. And part of that is stemming at this ideological flourishing that is occurring within families. And Chairman Royce and myself earlier this year held a hearing on the importance of women in battling violent extremism, and the name that you mentioned, Farah, in terms of Sisters Against Violent Extremism came up. I know you touched on it in your testimony.

But women are the first educators of their children. They are in a unique position to spot signs of radicalization and extremism, and they are also in a very pivotal position to try and deal with that. And I think we have to empower women to recognize this, to recognize the signs, and give them tools as to how to deal with that.

But could you comment on the Sisters Against Violent Extremism and the overall effort to try and use women more effectively and mothers more effectively in this fight against extremism, and to really, you know, quash this ideological growth?

Ms. PANDITH. Thank you very much for that question.

You know, I talked a lot about the ideology and where it stems, and I don't need to explain to all of you how important family is. And as a young person grows up, this question of identity, the confusion, asking questions, these millenials are experiencing something that no other generation has experienced, and in the context of a post-9/11 world, that is why I said the numbers are massive. You know, one-fourth of the planet is Muslim; you know, 1.6 billion people. Sixty-two percent of that number is under the age of 30. These are millenials that have grown up looking at their life in a very different way. Everybody has an identity crisis, okay, it doesn't matter what religion you are, but something specific is happening to a generation that has grown up in the context of 9/11, asking questions that their parents and their grandparents didn't ask.

And as they are dealing with this sense of identity and belonging, they are looking for answers, and the answers that they always go to are not traditional, necessarily. It isn't the cleric, necessarily. It is not the elder person in the village town or city. It is Sheikh Google who answers a lot of these questions for them.

The reason why women are important is for two reasons: One, as you said, the mothers are the child's first teachers, they are seeing things with their children, they are beginning to see changes happening. If you are looking at some of the radicalization processes and you go back and you talk to the parents, they have seen signs, mothers talk about things that they have seen. They influence the ecosystem within the home. Very, very important.

But there is another piece of this, and that other piece of this is how you use women to mobilize their perspective globally and connect those things. That is where we began to look at models that would work on a grassroots level that are very local and are inspired by regular people. It wasn't Government coming in and saying something.

In the Bush administration, we looked at the model of Mothers Against Drunk Driving here in America and said, how did that get off the ground? How do we begin—how do we build this? And we began to think about what would happen if we began to build a network of like-minded women who could push back against extremist ideologies, and seeded Sisters Against Violent Extremism with an incredible woman named Edith Schlafer in Vienna, and gave her a small seed grant to get this off the ground and asked her to move it forward.

Right now, you know, all these years later, it is an independent organization that has chapters all over the world, but she has mobilized and built a network of women to push back, to talk about things, to put the lessons that she has learned on the table.

That is one piece of the complexity with women and extremism. Okay. The other is what is happening to Muslim women. And that is the other piece, if you wouldn't mind, I will just spend a moment on.

Mr. KEATING. No. I think that was my second question, so you are heading the right direction.

Ms. PANDITH. Okay. So in my role as Special Representative to Muslim Communities, one of the most impressive points to me was that what I thought had happened in Europe, this identity crisis, was not just minorities living in Europe, but, oh, my goodness, that was happening to Muslims in Muslim-majority countries as well.

So this idea that identity crisis from Malaysia to, you know, Argentina with Muslims matters to us, and it matters very boldly, because as people are asking these questions, as I said, the vacuum is being filled by narratives that come from extremists. That doesn't leave women out of the picture. These are digital natives, they are connected. With the swish of their finger on their, you know, smart phone, they are getting ideas that are bouncing around the world.

And what did I see as special representative? I began to see a change in the way this generation of young Muslim women began to think about themselves, think about their role. And so you are seeing a two-pronged thing: One, you can absolutely use women, and you should, to stop the stem of radicalization, to understand what is happening in the home.

The other point is we are beginning to see women getting radicalized in a——

Mr. KEATING. Oh, that was my question.

Ms. PANDITH [continuing]. In a very big way, right. So——

Mr. KEATING. If I could for a second. There is an irony there, because in many of these groups, the place of women is anything but high in the level of authority and power; however, you are seeing ISIL and some of these other groups use women, not necessarily as soldiers, but you are seeing them used in the social networking and communication and in shaping people's ideology in countries where some of the people—the average age of some of these countries, the average age is 25 years old.

So that if you could just continue, I think that was the second point I wanted to make.

Ms. PANDITH. Well, of course. You are correct. And that age group is really pivotal, because they are beginning to be mothers themselves, they are raising their children a particular way, they are thinking about their role in society in a particular way. Either you are going to be open and engage with the outside or you are going to retreat and come back in. So you are looking at data points across the board.

You are also looking at what they are looking at online, what they are listening to, how they see themselves. It doesn't take a lot of imagination. This summer, ISIS has an all women's, you know, organization. We have AQ doing the same thing. If we use our imagination and think of what else comes down the pike, it is very scary.

Mr. KEATING. Yeah. I will just bring one point home, Mr. Chairman, and that is the point that even in the Boston Marathon bombing——

Ms. PANDITH. Yes.

Mr. KEATING [continuing]. It is very clear the effect that Tamerlan Tsarnaev mother had on his radicalization. I won't comment on, since there is a trial pending, on the, you know, her other son, but I will say clearly with Tamerlan, that has been proved.

So Mr. Chairman—thank you for your comments. Mr. Chairman, I yield back.

Mr. ROHRBACHER. Thank you. Yes. And thank you for your thoughtful questioning.

And Mr. Yoho.

Mr. YOHO. Again, thank you, Mr. Chairman. I thank you both for your testimony.

And, Mr. Joscelyn, I think you are right on. I mean, we are seeing this happening now. And you were saying most of the radicals don't come back. We don't need most of them. If you go back to 9/11, we all know there were only 19 people, and they had, I think, it was $500,000, but they were able to change real quickly.

And now we have these organizations that have become more coalesced. And what I have seen, and correct me if I am wrong, is an escalation of the amount of radical groups and I see them coalescing into a stronger force, well organized, well funded. With ISIL supposedly getting $3.5 million a day in the sale of oil on the black market, we are just going to see more and more of that.

And in this meeting room here, it was about 6 months ago, we had a group that was representing Somalians that had come to the United States. Minnesota is where they are from. And I asked them why they came to Minnesota. I was born in Minnesota and I was glad—it is a great state, but it is a little bit too cold for me, so why would the Somalians choose Minnesota, and they said it was for education and jobs. But yet when I asked them what percentage of the male population were employed, he said it was very low, it was high unemployment in that group. What percentage graduated from high school? He said it is very low. And then I went into, you know, the questions of how many are practicing

Muslim. I assume the majority. And he said yes. Then we moved on to do they follow Sharia law or U.S. constitutional. He says, we go with constitutional law, but, yes, Sharia. And then I asked him if they were assimilating and becoming Americans and adapting our ideologies. And he says, we are having a real hard time with that.

That scares me, because we are growing that type of thing that we are seeing now, and as you brought out, the person from Florida and the person before Minnesota going over and becoming radical jihads.

We have to have a way—and this goes back to a bigger problem, you know, with our immigration policy. I think we all want responsible immigration, but we have to do it right to bring the people over here.

But going back to the ISIL threat, removing the passports from these people, one of the questions I had is if we remove these passports—I lost my train of thought here. How can the U.S. help our European allies to defend themselves from the threat of these returning foreign fighters? You know, they got a Western passport, they can go over there and they can come back if they are a U.S. citizen. And I think Britain has already started to take these passports away. Is that right?

Mr. JOSCELYN. That sounds right. Yeah, they have—Britain has a number of security restrictions they can put in place.

Mr. YOHO. Okay. With that, I am going to yield back.

And, Mr. Chairman, I appreciate your time.

Mr. ROHRBACHER. Well, thank you very much.

A couple of questions. Are these the uneducated—overseas, are these the uneducated people of lower classes who can't get jobs or are they like Bin Laden from the upper crust, who are actually very well educated and not necessarily just the product of Madrassa schools, but instead, people who know the choices and have made the choice that their religion is better than everybody else's?

Mr. JOSCELYN. It cuts across socioeconomic boundaries. It is not easy to typify sort of your recruit in that regard. You know, when you look at, again, the common example are the suicide hijack pilots on 9/11: Highly educated, come from good families. You know, Bin Laden came from a good family, Ayman al-Zawahiri came from a very influential family. You find this over and over and over again.

It is really the strength of the idealogy that binds them together, and not necessarily any socioeconomic factors.

Mr. ROHRBACHER. Uh-huh. Let me note it before we move on, and that is that it is vitally important that we do not try to lump all Muslims into the category of terrorists, otherwise, we are doing exactly what the terrorists want us to do, which is create a dichotomy between the Western world and all Muslims, and thus expand dramatically their strength and potential danger.

So we should make sure we reach out—and again—and this is—Ms. Pandith, how—you were talking about the Muslim community and perhaps an identity crisis going on with different people. Do you think that there is a real threat that we could have an overreach here and push Muslims into the radical terrorism camp, and do you see that happening at all?

Ms. PANDITH. So I think one of the things that is important for us to understand is what we have learned over 13 years of trying to look at the radicalization process, what is happening in communities, what Government can do, what communities can do, how the strengths and weaknesses have played out over the course of 13 years. And you asked a really important question about, you know, who are these people, you know, how well educated are they, where do they come from.

One of the things I was talking about in my testimony is the nuanced approach to understand the distinction within—certainly here today we are talking about Europe. Which generation are we talking about? Which ethnicities are we talking about? How are they looking at the particular issues that they are dealing with?

The success is going to coming from the community level. And as you look at the responses across Europe and how governments are looking at the threat, there is a wide range of reactions to this growing problem, but when you are looking forward, when you are looking at the distant opportunities for recruitment, we have to start with the immediate family, we have to start with the communities, and we have to make sure that the communities are getting information about what we have learned about how recruitment happens, that we are looking very deep at all of these issues, and not sort of separating the immediate from, you know, just not having a threat now.

Mr. ROHRBACHER. You know, I will have to tell you, the world has faced many different challenges from murderous groups over the history of the plant. And Muslim extremism, or I should say, you know, and perhaps, I know a lot of Muslims don't like the—even the word ''Islam'' associated with radicalism, but a lot of us are having trouble with that.

We want to be respectful of their faith, but we can't help but notice that the people who are murdering people are doing so in the name of their faith, and it really pulls on a lot of us, because we know, I mean, I know many Muslim people who are wonderful people and would never dream of that, and I don't think their faith is doing anything but adding to their life, but obviously those people whom we are fearing now identity the Islamic faith, Muslim faith as the motivator that is motivating them to do that. They are announcing that to the world.

And I am not sure, and, again, after listening to your testimony, you know, 50 years ago and 60 years ago, the world was threatened by these Nazis, who had no Muslim connection at all, who were, basically came from a Christian country, and Japanese militarism, which had its own—you could identify the Shinto religion that they were part of that glorified their ancestors, especially, who were very military successful ancestors, you could see that direct line, but I don't—to be fair about it, I don't think that our—that the greatest generation that we call in the United States spent time trying to psychoanalyze why people became Nazis or why people of Japan backed up their militarist wing; we simply went out and had to defeat them.

And I think maybe that is where we are at now, that we want to understand, as you were saying, these Muslim people who are involved with the radical terrorist elements, respecting the fact that most Muslims are not that way, but the job now is not some long-term analyst, but instead, to try to defeat this evil force that would murder our families.

And maybe you both would have a comment on that?

Ms. PANDITH. Mr. Chairman, may I just respond to what you were saying?

Mr. ROHRBACHER. Sure.

Ms. PANDITH. In terms of the threats that our world have faced, you very nicely pointed out two ideological examples, but our country took it seriously, the ideological piece. We invested everything, both hard power and soft power, to defeat that threat. We have not done that now, sir.

Mr. ROHRBACHER. You know what? I don't think that we actually put any effort into denouncification until after we defeated them and disarmed them, and that is when we—denouncification had an impact, but it wasn't until then.

And right now, I think we are in the battle mode, of this fight, you know. And maybe afterwards, we can—and that is why we have to support the President in his efforts as best we can, and other—and unite as a country against this, because I happen to believe it will—and I think we all agree, that, yes, our European friends are now going to bear the brunt, but we are just the very next step away from there, and our children, our families are going to be at stake.

Mr. Joscelyn?

Mr. JOSCELYN. Well, I don't think it is necessarily an either/or. I agree with you that we need to defeat them militarily. I think the Jihadist ideology needs military successes in order to recruit, and so they need to be defeated militarily, otherwise they are going to deep saying that they are the strong horse people should side with.

But just take a step back for a second. And what is going on here is, I find, as somebody who has studied Bin Laden and Zawahiri very carefully, we still don't ever really understand what they were all about. You know, 9/11, these terrorist attacks, they weren't an end in and of themselves; they were trying to seek to spark a political revolution within the Muslim world. And within the Jihadi camp, Bin Laden is known as the reviving sheikh. And what does that mean? It means that, according to al-Qaeda's theory of the world, Muslims had—were no longer waging Jihad like they were supposed to, and he needed to revive the Jihadi spirit across the Muslim world.

Now, this becomes—that—so it becomes very much an ideological battle, because if you look at what they were trying to do, and, in fact, Bin Laden was a great student of the Chinese game Go, where you can convert pieces on the board to your side. Once you surround them and they become your pieces, and then you can re-deploy them. That is a political revolutionary thinking about how to convert Muslims to his cause, which is what al-Qaeda's always been about.

And they have had many setbacks in that regard, mainly because most of their violence has actually killed their fellow Muslims. And this is a strategic liability, not just for al-Qaeda, but also for ISIL. ISIL is you know, we are talking about the threats to the West right now, and we should be, but ISIL, if you look at their body count, right now it is a lot of Muslims throughout Syria and Iraq and only a few Westerners, you know.

And I have seen, you know, you talk about the beheading videos of James Foley and Steven Sotloff, which really galvanized us into action, I can tell you I watched probably hundreds of beheadings of Syrians and Iraqis before that, you know, Muslims on the ground who are our allies in this fight who were getting killed, you know. And so that is where the ideological battle is——

Mr. ROHRBACHER. Sure.

Mr. JOSCELYN [continuing]. Because in the military battle, you are talking about, Congressman, we need to figure out who our allies are. And we have a lot of Muslim allies. We have to identify them as such in this greater contest.

Mr. ROHRBACHER. I think that is a—you have made a really—well, both of you have made really good points today. And the idea about keeping in mind that there have been more Muslims murdered by these—by the people that threaten us today than have Anglos or European background people, although obviously we are concerned about the safety of our families. And that is our job here, is to make—ultimately to be concerned about our families.

And hopefully our fellow Americans of the—and I would hope that we challenge, all of us challenge them to step up and back them up in their communities when they take a stand against these type of extremists that would murder their fellow human beings.

I was shocked when several organizations that I read some fliers from them suggesting—from several Muslim organizations in the United States were suggesting that their people not cooperate with the FBI. I don't know——

Mr. Keating, I don't know if you have seen that or not, but I certainly saw a couple of handouts indicating—I won't name the group, because maybe it is unfair to that group. Maybe that only reflected one or two people in the group who took advantage of a situation.

But we challenge our fellow Americans who are Muslims to join us and help us win this battle, because, as we are learning today, it is a—what is happening in Syria is going to be a wave that hits us here in the United States and is already beginning to be felt in Europe.

Let me ask Mr. Joscelyn about the shared threat that we have with our European allies, but do we not also share this threat, and I mentioned this in my opening statement. Do we not share this threat with Russia and should we not cooperate with Russia? Mr. Keating and I actually went to Moscow and met with their intelligence operatives and got a briefing on those people who were involved with the bombing in Boston, the Boston Marathon.

Mr. JOSCELYN. Well, I will preface this by saying there are a lot of ways in which our interests in Russia obviously are not consistent. We have divergent interests across the board I would say.

But, you know, to your point when you study who is in Syria right now, the Chechen Jihadists in Syria right now, these are not freedom fighters, you know. They are deeply opposed to the Russian Government. They are also hostile to us. They are very much on either ISIL's side or al-Qaeda's side in Syria. In fact, you know, this hearing is happening because of ISIL's military gains on the ground in Iraq and Syria.

One of the top military commanders in Syria is a Chechen for ISIL. His name is, he is known as Abu Omar al-Shishani. And he is actually the one who really gave them their military victories in eastern Syria, which has opened up the pathway into Iraq. And so the Chechen Jihadists are really the most committed, I would say, skilled and oftentimes tacticians in this fight. They are a threat to Russia, they are a threat to our interests, so in that sense there is a common threat there.

You know, one of the interesting things we were talking about the radicalization of women, well one of the biggest examples of that is in fact the Chechen black widows who have committed terrorist attacks in Moscow. These are the widows of fallen Jihadists in the Chechen and groups in Dagestan and Chechnya who go on to become suicide bombers in operations there. So there is a common bond at least in that one narrow sense in terms of the threat of the Chechen Jihadists.

Mr. ROHRABACHER. I notice our other witness shaking her head. Would you like to add to that?

Ms. PANDITH. Thank you, Mr. Chairman.

I also wanted to say, I mean, you made a very good point about having everybody join to push back against the ideology of extremists, and what you have seen in the last 13 years since 9/11 is the increase of voices that are pushing back that are coming from Muslim communities, and you are seeing new networks, you are seeing networks of former extremists that have been built to push back, but that needs to be ramped up. Those are the voices that matter, those are the credible voices, and to your point about Russia and the black widow example that my colleague has just raised, that is, to me that is a great illustration of, you know, the worst case scenario, but what we ought to be looking at is not when it is the tip of the iceberg; what is actually percolating? What is actually happening to get them there? And that is where we have to stem and cut the radicalization process. If you don't have recruits, you will not have armies.

Mr. ROHRABACHER. To be fair, I cannot understand why a religious extremist group that would, it appears on its surface to be so anti the freedom of women and so oppressive in terms of saying that women have to wear a garment and hide themselves and look out a little slit or can't drive cars or can't have regular jobs, I do not, I can't comprehend how there would be women joining the ranks of people like who held those beliefs in order to try to create a society based on those standards.

Ms. PANDITH. Mr. Chairman, there are lots of reasons why the women are joining the fight, and I know that there is not just one or two that are prominent. There are many, some of which include wanting, some of the married people who are there and want to be part of that ecosystem.

Some want to raise children so that they are creating the next army. Some do it because they are ideological, they are so invested in the ideology of building a so-called caliphate that they want to be part of this and they want to live there. I mean, there are many reasons why, but their sense of belonging in terms of where they are.

If you look at the two teenage girls from Austria who ran away from home to join Chechen Jihadis, I mean, this is an illustration of the kinds of things that are happening. How is it possible that two young girls who grew up in an open and free environment chose to do that? How did they get radicalized? What were they looking at online that moved them in that direction?

And sir, the last point I would say is the other role that women are playing is that enticement role. So if you have somebody on the other end of a You-Tube video or a chat room that is eager to bring women on board and you are another woman and her voice calling them in, it is very persuasive.

Mr. ROHRABACHER. Well, we obviously face a major challenge and not just with Democrats and Republicans uniting the face of foreign challenge, but also people of various religious faiths, including the Muslim community and the Christian community and Jewish community here in the United States and elsewhere.

We need to have some unity behind this to help save mankind from the senseless murder of innocent people, and when we talk about people being terrorists, their purpose is to terrorize, and that means to win the battle through terrorizing a population, to letting them achieve their goal through that terror.

We Americans are not going to be terrorized into giving up our rights and our freedom and our ability to be part of the world, and I don't—I think we need to stand with our European allies in this and especially our allies in the Muslim world who are being killed and murdered at a much higher rate.

Closing statement from Mr. Keating and Mr. Yoho?

Mr. KEATING. Thank you, Mr. Chairman.

I think what was interesting with this hearing, among many things, was how we were dealing with how this radicalization occurs, the stemming of it, how it is nurtured, and I think we don't put enough emphasis on that, and we are going to have to, and we can't just do it here in the U.S. We have to do it in Europe and we have to do it certainly through the Mideast.

I look at the examples of what they are doing and how sophisticated they are doing things, they are actually making great efforts, whether it is ISIL or other radicalized groups associated with al-Qaeda. They are destroying Muslim history in many senses, not just orally and passing it on, but actually through the destruction of artifacts and the destruction of antiquities, and they are profiting actually from the sale of those to help fuel their cause.

But in the process they are destroying it and they are creating a new narrative of their own that is not historical, is not traditional, it is not religious, so we touched on that, and as we go forward I think that is something we should put greater emphasis on.

And I want to thank our two witnesses for touching on those things today in their testimony.

Mr. ROHRABACHER. Thank you, Mr. Keating.

And Mr. Yoho?

Mr. YOHO. Thank you, Mr. Chairman.

Thank you both.

As we were talking about, and I am sure you have read the book by Samuel Huntington, The Clash of Civilizations, talking about the majority of the conflict in the world is Muslim to Muslim, but when you insert the Westerner, they come together, and we become the common enemy.

How much of the growth of radicalism comes from the hatred of the West ideals of liberties and freedoms versus the Western foreign policy or are they connected in your opinion?

Mr. JOSCELYN. Well, I will say the ideology is deeply anti-Western. A lot of times they view our foreign policy through a very conspiratorial lens which doesn't actually reflect reality.

So, you know, for example, even though we were on the side of Bosnian Muslims during the conflict there in the 1990s, you know, Osama bin Laden was able to rationalize critique of U.S. policy because we didn't deliver arms to Muslim forces quick enough.

Mr. YOHO. Right.

Mr. JOSCELYN. So it is deeply—it is more ideological than my view of being anti-Western than it is really foreign policy driven.

Mr. YOHO. Is it Ms. Pandith, right?

Ms. PANDITH. Yes.

Mr. YOHO. The girls that were in Australia, were they Australian background? Were they born there or are they of Muslim descent?

Ms. PANDITH. It was Austria. If I misspoke——

Mr. YOHO. I am sorry, Austria.

Ms. PANDITH. No, no, no, it is all right. I believe that they were born there. I can double check for you and get back to you on that point.

Mr. YOHO. Well, because what I see is the lone wolf starting to develop in this country like that Alvin—I think it was Ali Muhammad Brown who had supposedly murdered four American men in the name of Jihad against the West, and we just don't want to see that over here, so I look forward to dealing with you in the future and I hope——

Ms. PANDITH. It would be my pleasure.

Mr. YOHO [continuing]. To help design policies that will prevent this.

Thank you both. Have a great weekend.

Mr. ROHRABACHER. I want to thank the witnesses.

Thank my fellow colleagues.

The American people need to know that we are taking this very seriously and that there is a threat that is a merging threat with this battle that is raging in Syria, it will impact on our society and our safety. We have got to pay attention to it.

What the people in Europe are now beginning to experience are those people coming back from this conflict we will experience as well. The wave will hit us, and it is—what we do about it, we have to use our heads, but we have to be courageous, and again we need to make sure that all Americans, including Muslim Americans, are recruited in this effort. So I want to thank the witnesses and this hearing is adjourned.

[Whereupon, at 10:28 a.m., the subcommittee was adjourned.]

APPENDIX

MATERIAL SUBMITTED FOR THE RECORD

SUBCOMMITTEE HEARING NOTICE
COMMITTEE ON FOREIGN AFFAIRS
U.S. HOUSE OF REPRESENTATIVES
WASHINGTON, DC 20515-6128

Subcommittee on Europe, Eurasia, and Emerging Threats
Dana Rohrabacher (R-CA), Chairman

September 12, 2014

TO: MEMBERS OF THE COMMITTEE ON FOREIGN AFFAIRS

You are respectfully requested to attend an OPEN hearing of the Committee on Foreign Affairs, to be held in Room 2172 of the Rayburn House Office Building (and available live on the Committee website at http://www.ForeignAffairs.house.gov):

DATE: Friday, September 19, 2014

TIME: 10:00 a.m.

SUBJECT: Islamist Foreign Fighters Returning Home and the Threat to Europe

WITNESSES: Mr. Thomas Joscelyn
                 Senior Fellow
                 Foundation for Defense of Democracies

                 Ms. Farah Pandith
                 Fisher Family Fellow
                 Belfer Center
                 Harvard Kennedy School of Government
                 (*Former U.S. Special Representative to Muslim Communities*)

By Direction of the Chairman

The Committee on Foreign Affairs seeks to make its facilities accessible to persons with disabilities. If you are in need of special accommodations, please call 202/225-5021 at least four business days in advance of the event, whenever practicable. Questions with regard to special accommodations in general (including availability of Committee materials in alternative formats and assistive listening devices) may be directed to the Committee.

COMMITTEE ON FOREIGN AFFAIRS

MINUTES OF SUBCOMMITTEE ON _____ *Europe, Eurasia & Emerging Threats* _____ HEARING

Day_____ *Friday* _____Date___ *September 19, 2014* __Room_____ *2171* _____

Starting Time ___ *9:24am* ____Ending Time ___ *10:28am* _____

Recesses [____] (____to ____)(____to ____)(____to ____)(____to ____)(____to ____)(____to ____)

Presiding Member(s)

Hon. Dana Rohrabacher

Check all of the following that apply:

Open Session ☑   Electronically Recorded (taped) ☑
Executive (closed) Session ☐   Stenographic Record ☑
Televised ☐

TITLE OF HEARING:

Islamist Foreign Fighters Returning Home and The Threat to Europe

SUBCOMMITTEE MEMBERS PRESENT:

Rep. Keating, Rep. Poe,

NON-SUBCOMMITTEE MEMBERS PRESENT: *(Mark with an * if they are not members of full committee.)*

HEARING WITNESSES: Same as meeting notice attached? Yes ☑ No ☐
(If "no", please list below and include title, agency, department, or organization.)

STATEMENTS FOR THE RECORD: *(List any statements submitted for the record.)*

TIME SCHEDULED TO RECONVENE _____
or
TIME ADJOURNED ___ *10:28am* ____

_____
Subcommittee Staff Director